T0318837

THE PARENTS' GUIDE
TO
SECONDARY EDUCATION

THE PARENTS' GUIDE
TO
SECONDARY EDUCATION

BY

H. A. WRENN, M.A.

Headmaster of
Wellingborough Grammar School

CAMBRIDGE
AT THE UNIVERSITY PRESS
1953

CAMBRIDGE
UNIVERSITY PRESS

University Printing House, Cambridge CB2 8BS, United Kingdom

Cambridge University Press is part of the University of Cambridge.

It furthers the University's mission by disseminating knowledge in the pursuit of
education, learning and research at the highest international levels of excellence.

www.cambridge.org
Information on this title: www.cambridge.org/9781316612798

© Cambridge University Press 1953

First published 1953
First paperback edition 2016

A catalogue record for this publication is available from the British Library

ISBN 978-1-316-61279-8 Paperback

To

BARBARA

CONTENTS

ACKNOWLEDGEMENTS

I am deeply indebted to G. E. Churchill, M.A., Chief
Education Officer of Northamptonshire, for his kind advice
and to Miss J. Horton, B.A., Headmistress of the County
High School, Wellingborough, for information with respect
to the education of girls. I also thank the following gentle-
men for their kind assistance: J. H. Butler, B.A., J. Butter-
field (Loughborough), T. G. Cook, M.A., W. Henderson,
B.Sc., W. Holmes, M.Sc., A. Jackson, M.A., Ph.D., E. J.
Pfaff, M.A., H. C. Phillips, A.R.C.A., A. W. Leftwich,
B.Sc., I. J. Nicholas, M.A., R. V. S. Ward, B.Sc., and the
staff of the Cambridge University Press.　H. A. W.

CHAPTER I

THE NEW FRAMEWORK

The truism that greater opportunities bring greater responsibilities is particularly relevant to education today. Parents are confronted with developments offering new and exciting opportunities to their children, but it is the responsibility of the parents to understand the nature of these opportunities and to ensure that their children take advantage of them.

By the Education Act of 1944, free secondary education became the right of every child in England and Wales. It is the purpose of this book to describe the nature of this education and the opportunities which it offers, to provide in simple terms answers to the many problems confronting parents today, and to offer them the background information necessary to the important decisions which they have to make on their children's behalf.

The 1944 Education Act was the logical development of earlier advances in education, which had provided universal education of the elementary type, but which at the secondary stage had only made provision for the grammar schools and to a lesser degree for technical and senior schools.

Now, by virtue of the Act, there is a statutory system of education organized in three progressive stages, primary, secondary, and further education, a continuous educational process through which all children and young people will pass.

At the primary stage no problem for parents of a selective nature exists, except in so far as considerations of a religious nature may influence the choice of school, or parents may prefer through the medium of the private preparatory school an alternative to the state system. It is at the secondary stage that the crucial question of choice emerges. In the words of the Act, 'the Minister and local education authorities shall have regard to the general principle that, so far as is compatible with the provision of efficient instruction and training and the avoidance of unreasonable public expenditure, pupils are to be educated in accordance with the wishes of their parents'.

In the state system of education the choice at the secondary stage lies between the grammar school, the technical, and the modern, and it is probable that for some years to come many parents will tend to prefer a selection in that order. Ultimately, however, with the expansion and full equipment of the technical schools and the building of new modern schools, it will be possible for a choice to be made in which the ability and aptitude of the child will be the only governing factors.

The traditional outlook of the grammar school has been to follow a curriculum of the academic type leading directly to studies of university standard. As such, the grammar schools, with the public schools, have provided recruits for the Church and State, the Services, the professions and the black-coated occupations.

In more recent years, however, the growing importance of the sciences and foreign languages, the introduction of such subjects as economics, and the gradual correlation of school work with the needs of society, have made the grammar schools a major field of recruitment for industry and commerce.

Although, therefore, a grammar school education may still lead directly to the university, classical studies have largely given way to modern, and the ever-increasing demand for mathematicians, chemists, physicists, biologists and economists plays a vital part in shaping the curriculum.

Significant as these changes may be, the primary function of the grammar school remains unaltered. Its purpose is to teach its pupils to think, to distinguish the true from the false, to accept valid premises and to build logically upon them. It is not the aim of the grammar school to prepare the pupil for any particular trade or vocation, but rather to train his mind so that he may face a variety of problems and adapt himself to changing circumstances.

For this work a special type of intelligence, capable of abstract thought, analysis and deductive reasoning is required. It is, therefore, only to be expected that the grammar schools should cater for a relatively small proportion of the population.

The aims of the technical school differ radically from those of the grammar school. Here the accent is not on scholarship, but craftsmanship. The curriculum, comprising as it does such subjects as engineering, building, metalwork, woodwork, bears a sharper relation to the eventual employment of the student.

This does not mean that the mind is not trained as well as the hand and eye. Mathematical theory must go hand-in-hand with engineering, the principles of physics underlie the work of the electrician, and abstract art enters the sphere of design. It is merely that the emphasis is on the practical rather than the theoretical.

Here again the proportion of students attending the technical schools is relatively small, but this is due not so much to the specialized gifts required of the pupil as to the limited number of such schools in existence. The nation has now recognized the urgent need of expansion in this field, and it is certain that in the future an increasing number of young people will enter the technical schools.

The majority of children, however, will receive their secondary school education in the modern schools. Here we have a comparatively new field of education, combining to a degree the virtues of both grammar and technical school, while avoiding their insistence on specialization.

Many of these schools exist at present more in name than in reality, but progress is swift, and already sufficient new and generously equipped modern schools are in operation to show that we are on the threshold of a third form of genuine secondary education.

It is indeed vital to the nation that this should be so. For a freedom-loving and politically conscious democracy a high level of education in all walks of life is of paramount importance. On the modern schools in large measure rests the future prosperity of the country.

Outside the state system, but linked in varying degrees with it, remain the independent public schools. Their value is twofold. They represent the heritage of culture, on which the state grammar schools have largely modelled themselves, and from which in due course the modern schools may also draw inspiration. They are also a living expression of individualism in education which constitutes a valuable safeguard against the possible danger of stagnation inherent in a state-controlled system.

It is true that they are to a significant extent the preserve of the wealthier section of the community, but this weakness is tempered by the fluid nature of modern society and by the willingness of the schools themselves, in co-operation with the state, to draw their pupils from all classes.

Stretching beyond the secondary stage is the realm of further education, the translation into practice of the modern belief that education is not simply a limited period of preparation before the workaday life begins, but a continuous, ever-expanding experience, a fundamental aspect of life itself.

Further education may take many forms. For some it means the university and post-graduate research, for others it means a part-time continuance of instruction related to a career which has already begun, for yet others it is a voluntary widening of horizons as an antidote to the monotony of repetitive processes in modern industry. For all it will stimulate that intellectual curiosity without which no nation can flourish in the highly competitive world of today.

This then is the overall picture of the fabric created by the Education Act of 1944. A progressive society such as our own can provide the framework for opportunity, but only the individual can avail himself of it. In the case of education the individual is the child, but the child cannot plan for himself. That is the privilege of the teacher, and above all of the parent.

CHAPTER 2

THE ANNUAL ENTRANCE EXAMINATION

SELECTION OF PUPILS FOR SECONDARY SCHOOLS

This examination is open to all children between the ages of 11 and 12 or thereabouts on a given date of each year. In some cases children of 10+ are permitted to enter, if their head teachers vouch for their exceptional ability.

As a result of the examination, selected pupils are offered free places at grammar schools and in some areas at technical schools and at selective central schools. In such areas the following information concerning entry to grammar schools will be equally applicable to the others.

It is important to note that the examination is not restricted to pupils of the state primary schools. Pupils of private schools are equally eligible and frequently take the examination as a form of insurance.

A pupil who has been thus selected for a place in a grammar school can normally avail himself of that right in subsequent years, should the parents' circumstances alter and removal from a private or public school become necessary. Similarly, if parents move to another district, the pupil who has passed the annual entrance examination is entitled to a place in the nearest available grammar school.

The examination is generally conducted by a panel of examiners appointed by the local education authority. It is not conducted by the grammar schools themselves, although a part of the examination may take place on their premises. The marking of examination scripts is similarly undertaken by markers appointed by the local education authority, as is the final selection of the successful candidates.

For those candidates who are prevented by illness or other circumstances from taking the examination at the proper time a further opportunity of so doing is often arranged. The examiners are also empowered to consider special pleas by parents and head teachers on behalf of children whose education has suffered through no fault of their own, and such representations should be made in writing to the Chief Education Officer of the local education authority concerned.

Some authorities have a further scheme for the inter-change at age 12 + or 13 + of the occasional pupil, who proves unsuitable for the grammar school type of education, with the pupil who, although unsuccessful in the annual entrance examination, has developed well subsequently along academic lines.

The form of the examination varies from one local education authority to another, but generally consists of the following:

An intelligence test.
English.
Arithmetic.

Candidates are graded by the head teachers of their primary schools, and this grading, together with their school record, is usually taken into account. In many cases there is also an interview in which the examiners seek to discover whether the candidate's abilities are suited to the academic nature of grammar school education. This object is generally achieved by simple comprehension tests and by friendly discussion about the candidate's interests.

(i) THE INTELLIGENCE TEST

(a) *Its value*

The value and purpose of intelligence tests are frequently misunderstood. It was believed at one time that, whereas the ordinary type of written examination favoured the pupil who had received the most thorough preparation, the intelligence test could give a truer assessment of his real ability.

Research has shown, however, that the intelligence test equally is susceptible to coaching, and that the more systematic the coaching the greater the effect. It is, therefore, unreliable to compare the scores of pupils with different amounts of previous experience of the tests.

Investigation has also shown that not only are substantial gains made by practising the tests, but that this acquired ability persists for many months. The gains are sufficient to invalidate comparison for examination purposes, and the provision of a preliminary practice test before the real examination does not entirely offset the effect of constant practice by the more fortunate pupils. Moreover, the mean intelligence quotient of sample groups of children differs considerably in various parts of the country.

The intelligence test is not, therefore, in its present stage of development an infallible guide to suitability for a grammar school education, particularly as it takes no account of character, outlook and background. Nevertheless, it is valuable in certain respects.

If the I.Q. is low, it can be reasonably assumed that the pupil, however willing, will be unsuitable for the type of work done in such schools and would be better off elsewhere.

Similarly a high I.Q., accompanied by low marks in the

English and Arithmetic examinations, would suggest some earlier handicap in the pupil's career and would invite further investigation.

Parents are advised not to attach too much importance to the results of intelligence tests conducted by magazines, commercial advertisers, etc. Unless the mean and standard deviations are similar, no valid comparisons can be made.

(b) Its nature

The test is usually preceded by a preliminary test, similar to the real test, which acts as a shock-absorber. This practice test does not count in the selection of the pupils.

The test proper normally lasts forty-five minutes. It frequently consists of a hundred simple questions, requiring a one-word answer or the underlining of a word in a number of given replies. When the tests have been marked, the scores are placed against a standardized table based on age and a converted mark is obtained accordingly. This mark is the intelligence quotient.

An I.Q. is, therefore, a measurement of intelligence adjusted according to age. It represents in effect the pupil's mental age divided by his actual age. The average I.Q. is 100. Thus, if a pupil of 10 years can do what the average pupil of 11 can do, he should have an I.Q. of $\frac{11 \times 100}{10} = 110$. Similarly the pupil of 12, who can only do the same, should have an I.Q. of $\frac{11 \times 100}{12} = 91$. Pupils with an I.Q. of 115+ are normally considered suitable for a grammar school education, but the position varies considerably from one area to another according to the general level of intelligence and the proportion of grammar school places available.

Typical questions in an intelligence test are:

1. Underline the word opposite in meaning to 'rapid' in the following: quiet, fast, sudden, slow.

2. Write the number which should come after the last of the following series of numbers: 13, 17, 21, 25.

3. In a code, $A = 5$, $B = 6$, $C = 3$, $D = 2$, what number equals $A \times B$? Which letter equals $D \times C$?

4. Fur is to cat as   are to parrot. Insert the missing word.

5. Why do animals have lungs? Underline the best answer.
   (a) In order to breathe.
   (b) To help them run quickly.
   (c) Because they are larger than birds.

6. All dogs have... (long hair, short ears, legs, puppies). Underline the word which makes the statement true.

7. December 1st is a Thursday. How many Sundays are there in the month? Which day of the week is Christmas Day?

8. It is midday and I am in England. As I walk along, my shadow is in front of me. In which direction am I walking? North, South, East or West?

9. If the letters of the word LEAP are mixed up and one other letter is added as well, we get the name of a fruit. What is the other letter?

10. John and William, Henry and Robert, Joan and Mary, are three sets of twins. John is younger than Henry and older than Joan. Who is the oldest of William, Robert and Mary?

11. Two of the following sentences mean nearly the same. Which are they?
   (a) His bark is worse than his bite.
   (b) He has a terrible temper.
   (c) He is not as unpleasant as he sounds.
   (d) He is not afraid of dogs.

12. The clock struck two when my watch said five minutes to two. I set the hands of the clock back ten minutes. What was the time by my watch when the clock struck three?

To answer a hundred such questions in forty-five minutes demands not only alertness but considerable powers of concentration. Nowadays, the sale of tests of this sort, such as the Moray House Tests, is generally restricted to local authorities and other examining bodies. It is possible, however, to purchase copies of tests used some years ago, which are not materially different from those in use today. They can be obtained at small cost from The University of London Press Ltd., Warwick Square, London, E.C.4.

(ii) THE ENGLISH EXAMINATION

This frequently consists of two papers:

Paper (1). Composition, e.g. completing a simple story, the beginning of which is provided. Composition is neglected by some authorities, despite its obvious test of creative ability.

Paper (2). Questions testing the pupil's command and understanding of words. Thus:

(*a*) A simple, descriptive paragraph containing alternative words of which the pupil must choose the one most suited to the context. E.g. 'Owing to the rain there were few (umbrellas, soldiers, spectators, linesmen) at the match', etc.

(*b*) A given list of words is followed by a series of sentences, each of which has a word missing. The most suitable from the list must be inserted.

(*c*) From a list of words the one nearest in meaning to a given word must be selected.

(*d*) As for (*c*) but phrases instead of words.

(*e*) A paragraph of narrative or description is given. Simple questions of fact are then based on it, together with questions as to the meaning of certain words or phrases.

(*f*) A simple sketch-map of a locality is given, and the pupil is asked to describe what would be seen on a certain route, etc.

(iii) THE ARITHMETIC EXAMINATION

This frequently falls into two parts:

(1) Simple questions of 'mental' or 'rapid' Arithmetic, such as:

(*a*) What is the cost of 2 dozen yards of wire at 3*d*. a foot?

(*b*) A customer gives a shopkeeper 2*s*. 6*d*. for 9 postcards at 2½*d*. each. How much change should he get?

(2) Harder Arithmetic, with questions such as:

(*a*) The cost of reserving seats at a theatre for 25 children is £4. 7*s*. 6*d*. Each child brings 6*s*. How much will he have left to spend after paying for his ticket?

(*b*) The ceiling of a hall is 35 ft. high. It has 12 electric lights hanging on chains, each 16 ft. 4 in. from the floor. What is the total length of chain used?

(*c*) A greengrocer buys 36 boxes of oranges at 53*s*. 6*d*. per box. He is allowed 1*s*. 9*d*. back for each box returned. If he returns 7 out of every 9 boxes, how much will he have to pay altogether?

(*d*) A train does a journey of 250 miles, and between stops travels at 45 miles an hour. The journey starts at 9.40 a.m. and finishes at 5.10 p.m. How much time is allowed for stops?

CHAPTER 3

THE COMMON ENTRANCE EXAMINATION (INDEPENDENT SCHOOLS)

Parents wishing to send their children to public schools normally apply to the school concerned several years in advance. Entry is then at 13 +, subject in most cases to a reasonable performance in the Common Entrance Examination.

This examination is held three times a year, in February, June and November, and can be taken either at the pupil's own preparatory school or at the school to which application is being made. Entry to the examination is made by application to the Secretary of the Common Entrance Examination Board.

Papers are set in the following subjects:

English (2 papers).
Mathematics (3 papers): Arithmetic, Algebra, Geometry.
Latin (2 papers): Translation, Composition and Grammar.
General (3 papers): Scripture, History, Geography.
French (2 papers): Translation, Composition and Grammar.
Greek (2 papers): Translation, Composition and Grammar; no longer compulsory.

Further information with regard to entry to the public schools, together with details of the entrance scholarships available, which are numerous and valuable, the fees, and the curriculum and facilities of the schools can be obtained in any public library from *The Public and Preparatory Schools Year Book*, published by A. and C. Black. Uniform with this volume is *The Girls' School Year Book*, which provides full information about both independent and maintained girls' schools.

Partial remission of fees is granted by many schools to members of various professions and the Services, and in this respect inquiry is best made directly to the school concerned.

Many social organizations have educational funds which may be used to assist their members, and some industrial firms provide similar assistance to employees.

Finally, although there is no rebate of income tax on the payment of school fees, a remission of income tax can be obtained by the use of the Educational Endowment or of the Deferred Insurance Policy.

CHAPTER 4

THE GRAMMAR SCHOOL

By the terms of the 1944 Education Act all schools provided by local education authorities are called 'county schools' and all non-provided schools are called 'voluntary schools'.

The latter fall into two classes:

(1) *Aided schools.* The governors being prepared to meet half the cost of alterations, improvements and external repairs, the remaining half is met by a direct grant from the Exchequer. The governors then retain two-thirds representation on the governing body as against one-third by the local education and minor authorities, together with the power to appoint teachers and to give denominational religious instruction.

(2) *Controlled schools.* The governors not being able to meet half the above costs, the local education and minor authorities have two-thirds representation on the governing body, and the local authority assumes all financial obligations. The power of appointing staff passes largely to the authority, and religious instruction is in accordance with an agreed syllabus, undenominational in character. The Foundation Governors may, however, arrange denominational religious teaching for pupils whose parents so wish.

There are no fee-payers in the county and voluntary schools. Free places are awarded on the basis of the annual entrance examination.

(3) *Direct-grant grammar schools.* This type of school receives a capitation grant from the Ministry of Education,

in return for which it must offer not less than 25 per cent of its places to non-fee-paying pupils from grant-aided primary schools, who may be selected by the governors or selected and paid for by one or more local education authorities. It must also put 'reserved' places at the disposal of the local education authority of the area served by the school, which will pay for them. The total of free or reserved places need not exceed 50 per cent. The school may charge approved fees to the remainder of its pupils, but they must be selected on their ability. Parents of these children may apply for remission of fees in accordance with an approved income scale, and the Ministry pays the difference between the fees actually paid and the approved fee.

The local education authority normally awards the places which it controls by means of the annual entrance examination in the same way as at the county and voluntary schools.

In all other respects the governors of a direct-grant grammar school remain largely autonomous, although the local authority is represented on the governing body.

(i) BOARDING SCHOOL EDUCATION

Mention has already been made of the principle underlying the 1944 Education Act that 'so far as is compatible with the provision of efficient instruction and training and the avoidance of unreasonable public expenditure, pupils are to be educated in accordance with the wishes of their parents'.

Many parents for varying reasons desire their children to have a boarding school education, and, although the proviso with respect to public expenditure limits the extent to which this desire may be satisfied, some provision for the purpose does exist. Not only do some local authorities control schools which possess boarding accommodation, but a few administer their own boarding schools. These are chiefly intended to accommodate the grammar school type of pupil, but occasionally there is provision for the modern school pupil. In addition some authorities have an arrangement with the independent boarding schools by which a few pupils may be selected each year for a boarding school education.

The following considerations are generally applicable to such selection, although they are by no means the only ones:

(1) Adequate but not necessarily exceptional attainment.

(2) Personal qualities of temperament.

(3) The lack of satisfactory home life, owing to such factors as lack of parental guidance, unsatisfactory conditions in the home, size of family, etc.

(4) Distance of the pupil's home from a suitable school.

Full boarding and tuition expenses may be met in necessitous cases by the authority together with grants for clothing and pocket-money, but a parental contribution may be required according to a sliding scale based on income. In some cases minor incidental expenses not met by the authority have discouraged parents from availing themselves of the scheme, and the allotted places have not all been taken up.

When a child does proceed to an independent boarding school by virtue of the scheme, it is generally understood that his or her education should continue until the age of 18.

(ii) CURRICULUM

The subjects taught in the grammar school are normally chosen from the following groups:

(1) *English Subjects*. English, History, Geography.

(2) *Languages*. (*a*) Modern: French, German, Spanish. (*b*) Classical: Latin, Greek.

(3) *Mathematics*. Arithmetic, Algebra, Geometry, Trigonometry, and, at a later stage, Calculus.

(4) *Sciences*. Chemistry, Physics, Biology.

(5) *Other Subjects*. Art, Music, Economics, Civics, Current Affairs, Handicraft, and for girls, Domestic Science, Needlework.

In addition every pupil has at least one period of Divinity weekly, except when debarred on religious grounds, and a few periods of Physical Training and Games.

The usual practice is for pupils in their first year or two to study a very wide syllabus. Later, as the pupil shows a leaning towards one or more groups of the above subjects, a system of options comes into force which enables him to give more of his time to those groups at the expense of the others.

As he approaches his fifth year at school, when he is likely to sit for the General Certificate of Education (G.C.E.), he will reduce slightly the number of subjects studied in order to have sufficient time to reach the required standard.

The new pupil direct from the primary school should not be allowed to worry because he finds a new subject difficult. The probability is that he will, under the system of options, discard this subject at a later date. In the meantime, if he does his best, he will gain in balance and experience.

It should always be remembered that several of the subjects studied by any particular pupil will not be directly used in his ultimate career. Their value is in training him to overcome difficulties, to think logically and constructively, to differentiate between the true and the false, and to become a good citizen.

Religious education

The 1944 Education Act provides that in county and voluntary schools the school day shall begin with collective worship on the part of all pupils, and that religious instruction shall form a regular part of the school syllabus. A pupil may, however, at the request of the parent be excused attendance at such worship or instruction, and, if the parent wishes him to receive religious instruction of a kind not provided in the school, he may be withdrawn from school either at the beginning or end of the school day for such time as is necessary to receive the instruction.

The Act also requires that the collective worship shall not be distinctive of any particular religious denomination, and that religious instruction shall be in accordance with an agreed syllabus adopted by the local education authority and shall not include any catechism or formulary distinctive of any particular religious denomination.

These provisions establish the legal minimum, but clearly the religious element in the life of a school is its most important. It is the element above all which bears directly on conduct and character, and as such should permeate the life and learning of the school as a whole. It is recognized, therefore, that the intention is not merely to provide instruction but to foster a Christian atmosphere in the school, and the agreed syllabus is not so much a hard and fast scheme of actual lessons as a guide and as material which can be freely adapted to the needs of the pupils.

With these considerations in mind the parent may care

to examine in detail the scheme compiled for pupils of secondary school age in a typical syllabus, *The Cambridgeshire Syllabus of Religious Teaching for Schools* (1949), published by the Cambridge University Press.

For the purpose of this book it is sufficient to note that the broad lines of study are as follows:

Age 11–13:

(*a*) *The life of Christ.* The aim is to draw into an integrated whole, all the parables, miracles and stories of Jesus with which the children have become acquainted in the junior stage. The study of Jesus' teaching will be reserved for the later age of adolescence, when questions and problems about God are more naturally of interest and concern. The aim here is to present as complete a picture as possible of Jesus as a person, and to give reality to the portrait.

(*b*) *Outstanding events in Old Testament history.* An outline knowledge of Old Testament history, right up to the time of Christ, is given, so that Jesus can be seen as coming into a real world with its own problems; so that the current ideas underlying his teaching may be understood in their context; and so that the picture can be shown of a people who recognize God as active in their history and as working out his plans for men.

Age 13–15:

(*a*) *The Gospel of Jesus Christ.* The Gospel story is traced, first, as the fulfilment of the Jewish hope that God would send a deliverer to vanquish the power of evil and establish the perfect rule of God; secondly, to show the universal character of the Christian message and its application to all circumstances and all times.

A clear and positive account of Jesus' teaching is given, which will encourage the pupil to express his own thoughts and relate the teaching to his own life, and examples are given of the lives of great Christians.

(*b*) *The development of ideas about behaviour, man and God in the Old Testament.* The aim is to inform the pupil about the function of the Old Testament prophets and about the social and moral problems with which they were concerned. The close relation between the Old and New Testaments is shown by tracing the gradual development of religious ideas leading up to the supreme revelation in the person of Jesus Christ. Some account is also given of the way in which the Bible has reached us and of the manner in which the authors and compilers of the books came to compose their work.

English

The English teaching endeavours to train the pupil (*a*) to utter thoughts in speech or writing intelligibly and effectively, (*b*) to comprehend, analyse and summarize the substance of written or spoken English, (*c*) to develop habits of discrimination and criticism in language, (*d*) by studying suitable literature to add to his ideas and introduce new avenues of study and appreciation.

Grammar is studied, but less as a subject in its own right than as a basic requirement in the art of composition. Through poetry, plays and prose the treasure-house of English Literature is glimpsed and personal taste and style are influenced. Play-reading and acting develop individual powers of expression, public speaking and oratory are practised, and private reading and the intelligent use of libraries are encouraged.

Emphasis is laid on the belief that English is not merely a subject in the curriculum of interest chiefly to the non-scientific pupil, but a vital means of expression common to all subjects and to all walks of life.

History

The course normally deals with the story of the growth of Great Britain. This, taken in its widest sense, includes the country's political, economic and social history, the development of its institutions of government, industry, agriculture, trade, transport and so on. These, in turn, imply a general understanding of Western civilization and of the Empire.

At the beginning of the course British History is studied from early times to the Middle Ages. Use is made of local examples, Roman roads, Saxon churches, villages mentioned in the Domesday Book and similar illustrations which may diminish the sense of remoteness in time. The pupil then proceeds to a general survey of the development of modern civilization. This completes the early background work.

A more detailed study is then undertaken of important periods of English History, such as the Tudor, Stuart and Hanoverian, and above all of the social and economic changes of the last two centuries.

This, together with some knowledge of European History, enables the pupil to consider intelligently current problems at home and abroad.

In the Sixth Form the political and economic aspects of history are studied in greater detail, and the Americas and the Eastern countries complete the world picture.

Geography

The syllabus normally seeks to cover the geography of the entire globe, but the greatest emphasis is naturally laid on the British Isles and the Commonwealth, Western Europe and the Americas.

Considerable use is made of films and foreign periodicals. The practical interest of the student is fostered by the maintenance of weather records and the making of maps to illustrate current events, surveys of fields and of communities, and various forms of outdoor work. The work of the classroom is constantly correlated with contemporary events and the basic features of civilized life. The climate, soil, relief features and natural resources of countries are studied in relation to the trade and productive work of their inhabitants.

This subject is fundamental to a proper understanding of the modern world and clarifies for the student the value of other school subjects such as history, economics, foreign languages and the sciences.

Modern languages

The foreign languages most frequently taught in the grammar schools are French, German, Spanish in that order of popularity. A few schools offer Italian or Russian. The general practice is for every pupil to study one foreign language, usually French, and for some pupils to tackle a second.

French is perhaps the most difficult of the three more popular languages, but the proximity of France and the high level of its national literature are factors likely to maintain its pre-eminence in the schools. German is somewhat easier to learn and is of particular value to intending scientists. Spanish is the easiest of all, especially at the elementary stage, and is readily tackled by non-linguistic pupils. As, after English, Spanish is the most widely spoken language in the world, its commercial value is considerable.

Although the grammatical structure of the foreign

23

language is carefully studied, the chief aim is to teach the pupil to speak and write it fluently. From the earliest stages oral work and free composition in the language are encouraged, and except for the teaching of grammar the direct method is preferred.

The study of literature is left to the Sixth Form, but some acquaintance with the better known authors is possible at an earlier stage. Exchanges and correspondence with foreign pupils, newspapers, magazines, gramophone records and wireless broadcasts are familiar stimuli in the modern teaching of foreign languages.

Latin

The study of Latin in grammar schools is usually confined to the abler pupils, for in the short time available it is too difficult a language for those of only average ability to be able to gain any positive sense of achievement. For those whose aim is a university course it is frequently an essential subject. Oxford and Cambridge require a pass at Ordinary Level in the G.C.E. from both Arts and Science students, and the other universities require Ordinary or Advanced Level from their Arts students.

The learning of Latin, which, as an inflected language, is in structure so unlike our own, provides a strong mental discipline and inculcates the habits of accuracy, concentration and logical thought. At a time when the teaching of formal grammar is so unfashionable, the Latin lesson can fill the gap, and, together with the study of derivations and essential meanings, can be a great help towards the correct and intelligent use of English.

It should be the aim of the Latin course not only to deal with the purely linguistic side, but also to give some introduction to Roman literature and Roman history, and to make some assessment of the contribution which Roman character and thought have given to the modern world.

Greek is also studied in schools, but usually only by those students intending to concentrate on Classical studies.

Mathematics

This is a most important subject in the curriculum, as it gives thorough exercise in accurate and systematic thinking, it permits the wider application of the ideas and principles of the sciences, and it has a direct bearing on most careers in a modern economy.

The school course follows roughly the chronological development of Mathematics in the history of man. The pupil will, before reaching the grammar school, have practised elementary Arithmetic and the simpler measurements and space relationships of Geometry. He now develops from Arithmetic the study of Algebra. In Geometry he begins to reason deductively about simple geometric shapes, and then to argue logically from agreed fundamental axioms. From Geometry, Trigonometry is developed, enabling calculations to be made within a wide range of practical problems of measurement. Arithmetic is continued in order to acquire facility with number relationships. Somewhat later in his school career the pupil will also use Calculus to solve problems of change.

Physics, Chemistry, Geography and Art are subjects whose content demands some knowledge of Mathematics, and the mathematical ideas involved are included in the course.

The techniques thus acquired, although adequate for the general range of careers, are relatively simple, and for the specifically mathematical or scientific career much more remains to be done in the Sixth Form.

Chemistry

The study of Chemistry expands the knowledge of, and helps to explain, many of the phenomena in everyday usage and also in nature. It is both cultural and utilitarian and gives training in scientific method. The pupil learns to observe the important results and discount the non-relevant and less important facts. He expands his knowledge of the science by doing personal experiments and making his own observations. By his experience he devises experiments to demonstrate principles. Practical Chemistry develops dexterity, initiative, and accuracy in manipulative work. The pupil learns to be critical and to accept facts determined as a result of his observations. The early stages are affected by the instinct of curiosity, and this is fostered and developed as much as possible.

In the first year, the syllabus is arranged to give a broad outline of the subject. The early lessons enable the pupil to become familiar with chemical apparatus and technique. A study is made during the first year of the elementary facts concerning crystals, common solvents, metals, non-metals, elements, oxygen, hydrogen, air, water, the mineral acids and common bases. In the second year the pupil is introduced to the atomic theory and the writing of chemical equations and formulae. A general study is made of carbon dioxide, limestone, the methods of forming salts, the allotropes of sulphur, sulphides and hydrogen sulphide, sulphur dioxide and trioxide, and sulphuric acid. Many of the mathematical parts of the syllabus are dealt with in the third year when the pupil can deal more easily with equations and arithmetical problems. In this way, equivalents and volumetric analysis are introduced into the syllabus. A study is also made of chlorine, hydrochloric acid, nitric acid and nitrates, ammonia, the oxides of nitrogen, carbon monoxide and fuel gases.

Consolidation and amplification of the work done in the first three years are the chief aims of the fourth and fifth years' study, with special attention paid to the syllabus required for the G.C.E. (Ordinary Level). In the Sixth Form the syllabus used is that required for the G.C.E. (Advanced Level). Here the pupil makes a study of Inorganic and Physical Chemistry. For the practical side of the work he is required to do volumetric and qualitative analysis.

Physics

Physics is the study of natural phenomena usually concerned with the behaviour of substances and specific objects when under the influence of forces and energy. It is thus distinct from Chemistry, which is largely concerned with the combination and action of one substance with another.

The subject-matter falls logically into the following groups:

(1) *General physics*. The laws governing the movement of objects, the equilibrium of objects at rest, the efficiency and power of machines.

(2) *Heat*. The effect of heat energy on substances, on the temperature and size of objects; the transfer of heat energy from place to place; heat engines.

(3) *Light*. The nature of light. Colours, mirrors and lenses, optical instruments.

(4) *Electricity and magnetism*. The generation of electricity, and its use in heating, lighting, motive power, and communications.

(5) *Sound*. The nature of sound; musical instruments.

The course during the first few years of the grammar school is an exploratory survey of natural phenomena, intended to make the pupil aware of the phenomena and to instil a desire to seek explanations. Later the course becomes more quantitative, showing how man has experimented, explained, and then applied the knowledge he has acquired. The work of the Sixth Form is largely occupied with a quantitative treatment of the subject-matter, together with training in careful measurement, experimental investigation, and correlation of observed facts—the basis of original work through which science advances.

Biology

The course in Biology has a twofold aim, first, to interest the pupils in the natural history of the living objects around them; and, secondly, to prepare the more advanced pupils for certain professional occupations.

Throughout the lower school, the course covers the basic facts underlying all forms of plant and animal life, as well as some knowledge of the working of the human body. The latter helps the pupils to take an intelligent interest in such matters as health and first aid, embracing, as it does, a study of the skeleton, the blood system, the principles of a healthy diet, and some knowledge of bacteria and disease. The former involves a study of plant life (of interest to the gardener), of bees and other insects, of fish, birds and a variety of living creatures. In many cases this is the beginning of a lifelong interest in nature which may become an absorbing hobby, especially for those living in the country.

The more advanced work done by pupils who specialize in Botany and Zoology in the Sixth Form gives them considerable practice in the dissection of animals and in the microscopic study of both animals and plants. It is equivalent to the first year course at a medical, dental or veterinary college and is designed for pupils who intend to take up these professions or the related subjects of Bacteriology, Pathology, Biochemistry, etc.

Art

This is a most important subject of the school curriculum, not only for the direct training of hand and eye and the cultivation of good taste, but for the simple, practical reason that everything which we make and use in everyday life has to be designed. It is well then that the principles of sound design and craftsmanship should be as widely understood as possible.

Many crafts can be practised at school, such as pottery, metalwork, printing, bookbinding, textile printing, weaving or embroidery. For less utilitarian design and for the graphic arts the normal medium is painting, but pen drawing, pastel, engraving, etching, lino-cutting are also practised.

The pupil's interest in Art is stimulated by excursions, illustrated talks and the study of objects of high artistic merit, whether actual or by photography, from all countries and all periods of history.

A course on the above lines provides a general cultural background for all pupils, and a useful beginning for the few pupils of particular aptitude who may then undertake in the Sixth Form and at a college of Art the highly specialized training required by the profession.

Music

The aims of music in school are to foster in the pupil a love for music, to provide him with as rich a store as possible of fine music, and to endow him with the means of widening his musical experience later in life.

The most effective method of attracting the pupil's interest is through performance, and the most easily available instrument is his own voice. Singing will, therefore, play an important part in the curriculum. In the junior forms it will be mostly unison singing, but the seniors will attempt part singing. The rudiments of music writing and reading are taught, which in turn provide the technical understanding of music necessary to its full appreciation at a later stage.

Performance of any kind is encouraged: the piano, the recorder, wind and string instruments, and ultimately the school orchestra. The pupil's store of music is also augmented by the use of gramophone and radio. As his knowledge of instruments grows he learns something of musical design.

Much of his classroom work is a preparation for out-of-school musical activities which both provide the individual with opportunities of self-expression and influence the musical awareness of the school in general.

Economics

This subject is frequently taught in the Sixth Form and is a development of work previously done in History and Geography. Basically it shows how man supplies his needs with the factors of production at his disposal, which are in the main labour and capital.

This involves a study of population (quantity and quality) and capital (man-made and natural), theories of employment and unemployment, and the real and potential economic progress of the nation. Theories of international trade show the means by which the standard of living of a nation may be raised, and this is measured by the construction and use of index numbers.

On the practical side the major industries of Great Britain in modern times are studied, together with economic developments in the Dominions and countries such as the United States, France, Germany and Japan. Economics gives the student a broader view of politics (economic policies put into practice) and therefore produces better-informed citizens. Most professional examinations, e.g. Banking, Accountancy, Law, etc., include a paper on economics; and advanced economics, backed by industrial experience, is a strong qualification for administrative posts in industry.

Domestic Subjects

Domestic Subjects form an integral part of the normal scheme of work for girls in secondary schools. In the grammar school they may be taken as subjects in the G.C.E. and fall under various heads: Cookery, Needlework, Housewifery and Laundry.

The subject provides a practical craft which most girls enjoy, and of which they see the ultimate value. The acquisition of any skill brings with it a sense of achievement, and this is particularly valuable for the less clever girl; the Domestic Subjects period provides a welcome change from bookwork, and here she finds the practical application of what she has already learnt in her science lessons, in art, and often in her social studies. Thus the subject bears a general relationship to the rest of the curriculum, and the Domestic Subjects lesson often affords a valuable means of inculcating the social graces.

There is a wide field of work open to the girl who wishes to specialize in Domestic Subjects. As long as she shows some practical dexterity, there is no need for her to have taken the subject in the G.C.E. before going to college, or even to have learnt it at school. It is desirable, however, that she should have passed the G.C.E., more particularly in such subjects as Physics, Chemistry and Mathematics. As well as training for teaching, there is the Diploma of Institutional Management, which qualifies for a great variety of posts in school, college, hospital and factory canteens, as matrons, cooks, housekeepers, organizers, dieteticians, demonstrators, etc.

Handicraft

Handicraft courses provide basic instruction in the theory and practice of woodwork, metalwork and technical drawing. The use of the drawing board, tee-square and instruments familiarizes students with drawings normally used in the crafts, and includes orthogonal projection and constructional details in the vertical and horizontal planes. The study of drawing and design is extended in the advanced courses. Theoretical work also deals with the history and development of the crafts, the nature and preparation of materials normally employed, and the use and maintenance of tools.

Knowledge gained in the theoretical classes is applied in the school workshops in the construction of common wood joints such as the dovetail, mortise and tenon, etc., and these are employed at a later stage in the construction of simple domestic furniture. Advanced students may also carry out a certain amount of decorative work. In the metalwork room, simple exercises involving filing, fitting and riveting are carried out, and the pupil also receives instruction in heat treatment, including hardening, tempering and annealing. Sheet metalwork with light materials requires the use of geometrical developments evolved by the pupil. In schools equipped with machines, students also have an opportunity to carry out suitable exercises on the lathe.

Boys who receive instruction in handicraft as outlined above may take the appropriate examinations in the G.C.E. at the Ordinary or Advanced Levels. The syllabuses provide an admirable preparation not only for boys who wish to make direct entry into industry, but also for those who wish to take up more academic or professional study. Such basic knowledge gives confidence, and, even if the boy is not aiming to be a craftsman, knowledge of the difficulties involved in the interpretation of theoretical ideas in a practical form is invaluable. Also, apart from the value of the instruction in preparation for a career, familiarity with the use of tools and materials has obvious domestic application and may also inspire a boy to take up a hobby which will be his lifelong interest.

Games and physical training

The primary aim of physical education is to provide the pupil with a wide experience of physical activity, which will so encourage his mental and physical development that he will look upon such activity as a tonic.

With this end in view the spirit of play is introduced as far as possible into all forms of physical training. In addition to the more popular games, such as rugby and association football, cricket, hockey, netball, tennis, swimming and athletics, many other games find a place in the schools, e.g. squash rackets, fives, boxing, wrestling, lacrosse, archery, rowing, badminton, basket ball.

Physical education is not merely an assortment of games and exercises, it is the basis for a way of life. It emphasizes the importance of hygiene, fresh air and sunshine, and a proper balance between work and recreation, between the mind and the body. It also teaches those principles of fair play and of the team spirit which are a vital part of all that is best in British traditions.

(iii) ORGANIZATION

The normal size of classes up to and including the Fifth Forms is about 30 pupils per class. Apart from other considerations this is the maximum number which can safely be supervised in a laboratory. In the Sixth Form with its wide choice of subjects, classes are generally much smaller.

According to the size of intake of first-year pupils, the school is thus reckoned as of one stream (30 pupils), two streams (60), three streams (90), etc. The organization of the streams varies between schools, but generally follows one of the following schemes:

(*a*) The streams follow approximately the same curriculum, but the pupils are selected according to ability and progress. They move from one stream to the other as a result of school examinations. The ground is covered more quickly in the A stream than in the B, etc. In many schools the A stream pupils will cover the normal five-year course to the Certificate year in four years, and then commence advanced work.

(*b*) Each stream has a subject bias. Thus one may give most time to languages and English subjects, another to Mathematics and the Sciences, etc. The pupils are selected according to preference and ability.

(*c*) The streams are parallel, and in those subjects taken by all pupils the classes are 'setted' according to ability.

Thus a pupil may be in the 'top' or 'bottom' set at any particular subject, irrespective of his Form.

Each of these methods has its virtues and its defects. From the parents' point of view, however, it is important to bear in mind the following points.

(*a*) In most schools the 'lowest' class in any particular year will receive as good teaching as the 'highest'.

(*b*) A pupil can only develop soundly when working at a speed suited to ability.

(*c*) The 'slower' pupil often obtains a more thorough grounding than the 'faster' pupil, if the work is taken seriously.

(*d*) The pupil who performed well in the primary school may find matters much more difficult when competing with pupils of equal ability in the grammar or high school. Signs of disappointment by parents when their child is no longer 'top' of everything are likely to undermine confidence still further.

(iv) THE GENERAL CERTIFICATE OF EDUCATION

It is normally expected that school pupils will take this examination at the age of 16 +, although the more able pupils may do so earlier, if the school considers it to be in their interest. Apart from this restriction, any person may take the examination, irrespective of age and previous education.

The full examination is held once a year only, from June to July, but there is another examination from November to December for Ordinary Level candidates only.

The following Examining Boards administer examinations and issue certificates to the successful candidates. These Boards do not set by any means the same syllabus in any particular subject, but the standard required is the same for all, and the certificates are of equal value.

University of Cambridge Local Examinations Syndicate. The Secretary, Syndicate Buildings, Cambridge.

University of Bristol. The Director of School Certificate Examinations.

University of Durham. The Secretary, School Examinations, King's College, Newcastle-upon-Tyne 2.

University of London, School Examinations Council. The Secretary, The Senate House, Malet Street, W.C. 1.

Universities of Manchester, Liverpool, Leeds, Sheffield and Birmingham Joint Matriculation Board. The Secretary, Joint Matriculation Board, 315 Oxford Road, Manchester 13.

Oxford Local Examination. The Secretary of Local Examinations, 12 Merton Street, Oxford.

Oxford and Cambridge Schools Examination Board, The Secretary, 10 Trumpington Street, Cambridge.

Examination Board for Wales. The Clerk to the Welsh Joint Education Committee, Cardiff.

A national Joint Examining Board representing the examining unions already functioning in various areas of further education is being formed in conjunction with the City and Guilds of London Institute. This body will also examine for the G.C.E. thereby providing part-time day and evening students with a preliminary qualifying examination to the professions and to degrees.

Students no longer at school but wishing to take a correspondence course (names of suitable colleges can be obtained at a Public Library) will be advised by these colleges of the most suitable examination board for their purpose.

The examinations are held at local centres, generally schools, lists of which are obtainable from the above. External candidates can usually arrange to take the examination at a nearby centre, and candidates in the Armed Forces can also take it at their stations under the supervision of the education officers of their units.

Copies of the complete regulations, including the syllabus, details of examination fees, etc., can also be obtained from the above, as can information about the purchase of examination papers set in previous years. The latter are obtainable from The Educational Supply Association Ltd., 181 High Holborn, London, W.C. 1. It is possible to obtain in one volume all the papers set in one year at either the Ordinary or the Advanced and Scholarship Level, or, in one booklet, a series of papers on one particular subject.

Candidates are examined at one or more of three levels:

(a) *Ordinary Level*. (This approximates to the old School Certificate credit standard.) Normally the pupil who is leaving school at 16+ and who does not intend to enter the Sixth Form will take all his papers at this level.

(b) *Advanced Level*. (This approximates to the old Higher School Certificate principal standard.) This level is for the pupil who has spent two years in the Sixth Form concentrating on his specialist subjects.

(c) *Scholarship Level*. This level is higher than the Advanced and is normally taken in the pre-university year by those candidates aiming at state scholarships.

The Examining Boards do not themselves award scholarships but report on the work of candidates to the various awarding bodies.

A candidate may not at the same examination enter for the same subject at different levels, but he may enter for different subjects at different levels.

A General Certificate of Education is issued to every candidate who reaches the pass standard in any subject at Ordinary or Advanced Level. The Certificates indicate the level at which the pass is obtained in the various subjects. Scholarship papers are not mentioned in the certificates, but candidates who reach Advanced Level standard in a subject taken at Scholarship Level have a pass in this subject at Advanced Level recorded on their certificates. A particularly good performance at the Advanced Level may also earn a 'Distinction' endorsement.

For the purpose of employment, exemption from professional examinations, etc., the value of a certificate naturally depends on the number, level and type of subjects it bears. Details of professional requirements are given in the section on Careers, pp. 62–79.

(v) THE SIXTH FORM AND UNIVERSITY ENTRY

The aim of the grammar or high school is to provide a continuous education from the age of 11 to 18, and an increasing number of parents are keeping their children at school after the age of 16, in order to give them the benefit of Sixth Form education.

They realize that, in addition to the intrinsic value of that education, the pupil's eventual prospects are enormously improved. This is true whether the pupil intends to go to a University or not. The Civil Service, for example, holds an examination for entry to the Executive Grade at age $17\frac{1}{2}$–$18\frac{1}{2}$, in addition to the Clerical Grade examination at age 16. Similarly commissions in the Services are obtainable through the Navy, Army, and Air Force Examinations at age $17\frac{1}{2}$–19. Many professions offer similar inducements to the Sixth Former, but particularly is this true for the scientific pupil, as the degree of laboratory training in the Sixth Form is so much higher than in the lower Forms.

Parents are sometimes unwilling to leave boys at school after 16, because they feel that it is vital to settle the boy in a career before he begins his national service at 18.

They overlook the fact that every boy and every employer is equally affected by national service. The post demanding the qualifications of the Sixth Former can only be filled by the Sixth Former.

On entering the Sixth Form the pupil will generally study three or four subjects with a view to offering them at the Advanced Level of the G.C.E. Other subjects will be discarded, assuming that the Ordinary Level has been satisfactorily passed.

The choice of advanced subjects depends on the pupil's ability and the general direction of his or her ambitions. The most frequent combinations of subjects are:

(1) English and two foreign languages. ⎫ Arts or Modern
(2) English, History and Geography. ⎭   Side
(3) Pure and Applied Mathematics, Physics ⎫ Science
and Chemistry. ⎬   Side
(4) Botany, Zoology, Physics and Chemistry. ⎭

But in a well-organized school almost any combination is possible, providing that it is sensible from the point of view of a career. Moreover, subjects not listed above such as Classical Languages, Economics, Art, Music, etc., are commonly taken at the Advanced Level.

For the intending industrial scientist, mathematician or engineer, (3) is the preferable combination of subjects. Normally (4) will only be chosen if the intention is to become a doctor, dentist, biologist, pharmacist or agricultural scientist.

As a result of the examination the successful pupil may qualify for exemption from the University Intermediate Examination, the award of a local education authority major scholarship and entry to a university.

University entry is normally obtained by application on the basis of the candidate's record. Oxford and Cambridge colleges often require boys to take an entrance examination and invariably do so in the case of girls.

Exemption from Matriculation in Great Britain and Northern Ireland (i.e. the minimum requirement for university entry) demands a G.C.E. showing five subjects of which three (including two at Advanced Standard) must be passed at one and the same sitting and must not all be related to one another, or six subjects (including two at Advanced Level) at more than one sitting. The subjects must include English Language, Mathematics or a science, a foreign language. Oxford and Cambridge also require a Classical language, but at the latter university the foreign language may be omitted if six subjects are offered. Oxford Matriculation is known as 'Responsions' and Cambridge Matriculation as the 'Previous Examination'. The corresponding requirement for entry to the Scottish universities is called the 'The Certificate of Fitness'. For further details of Matriculation and Faculty requirements application should be made to the Registrar of the university concerned or to the particular College at Oxford or Cambridge.

The requirement for the award of a local education authority major scholarship, payable if and when the pupil obtains entry to a university, varies as between authorities. A good performance at the Advanced Level in at least two subjects is generally looked for. The maximum grant payable is usually about £350 per annum for three or four years and varies according to the university and to the parents' income. The income scale recommended by the Ministry of Education is from £450–£2200 with allowances for dependents, school fees, insurance, mortgages, etc.

The same remarks apply to state scholarships, except that they are awarded on a competitive basis by the Ministry of Education and bring the holder somewhat greater honour. The highest honour is to win an open scholarship of a university. Full details of such awards are obtainable from the Registrars of the universities concerned. They are also listed in *The Public Schools Year Book*. The nominal value of these is not high, but if of £40 per annum or over, they are automatically supplemented by state scholarships on the same basis as above. In cases of hardship the local education authority will usually make a grant towards the expenses of a pupil who is sitting for an open scholarship at a university.

Intending teachers can no longer proceed to a university by means of a teaching grant, but must qualify by one of the above awards. If they do not wish to take a degree, they can, however, by application obtain a two-year grant tenable at a training college. The minimum requirement for entry is normally five subjects at the Ordinary Level.

Other scholarships available to students include those offered by the Lord Kitchener National Memorial Fund for the sons of those who have served in the Armed Forces, and those offered by Companies such as the Bankers, Brewers, Carpenters, Clothworkers, Cordwainers, Cutlers, Drapers, Fishmongers, Goldsmiths, Grocers, Haberdashers, Ironmongers, Leathersellers, Mercers, Skinners.

For students intent on a particular career there is a wide range of scholarships from Mining to Journalism sponsored by the industry or profession involved. An exhaustive list of such scholarships is given in *The Daily Mail Scholarships Guide*, obtainable in public libraries. Similar information is published in *The Student Chronicle*, the monthly publication of the National Union of Students, 3 Endsleigh Street, London, W.C.1, an organization capable of advising students on a multiplicity of subjects.

Finally, it may generally be assumed that any organization which disposes of funds for charitable purposes is willing to further the education of the sons and daughters of its members.

CHAPTER 5

THE PUBLIC SCHOOL

The information already given regarding the curriculum of the grammar school applies equally to the public school. In this respect it is probably true to say that the level of attainment in the grammar schools is so high that, viewed purely on the basis of the curriculum, there is little to choose between the two types of school.

The advantages of the public school arise principally from the boarding system. This system allows the school greater opportunity for training in leadership, cultural activities, games, and in promoting general moral and physical welfare. Moreover, there is ample time for the traditions and standards of the school to permeate the mind and character of the pupil.

An equally important consideration for many parents is that the tradition of the public schools is essentially Christian in character and that in some cases the foundation of the school derives from a particular religious denomination. Finally, many of the schools present a well-established record of preparation for individual professions or for the Services.

Information on these matters can be obtained in any Public Library from *The Public and Preparatory Schools Year Book*, which includes a valuable section on careers, mainly of the professional type, or similarly for girls in *The Girls' School Year Book*.

The Public Schools Appointments Bureau advises public schools and their members on the choice of careers.

Central Office: 17 Queen Street, Mayfair, W.1.

CHAPTER 6

THE SECONDARY TECHNICAL SCHOOL

(i) INTRODUCTORY

The secondary technical school is the natural development of the junior technical school, which did such valuable work in the years prior to the Education Act of 1944. These schools were usually established in technical colleges and provided a general education with emphasis on crafts and science. The course was normally of two or three years' duration, with entry at 12 + or 13 +. Boys trained in these schools were ideally suited to take up apprenticeships, particularly in the engineering and building trades, or to join the technical sections of the Armed Forces. Others entered H.M. Naval Dockyard Schools and achieved outstanding success. Similar schools were also run for girls, and these usually specialized in Commercial or Domestic Subjects.

At the present time, many secondary technical schools are still housed in the local technical college or in modified old buildings, and only a limited number have the advantages of new independent buildings. On account of these accommodation difficulties, it will be a long time before the Education Act is fully implemented, and many schools have no alternative but to carry on more or less in the tradition of the old junior technical school.

In general, however, it may be said that the secondary technical school differs from other types of schools in the possession of good workshop accommodation and equipment. Workshops for engineering, plumbing, bricklaying, carpentry, and painting and decorating provide opportunities for practical instruction in the crafts. Schools with commercial streams are also equipped with typewriters and modern office equipment. The instructors also differ from those found in other types of schools, in that they are frequently appointed after some years of industrial experience. Teachers with such a background can be a great asset, since they are able to pass on to the pupil the benefit of their own first-hand knowledge and experience. Some of our best craftsmen have been attracted to the teaching profession and are handing on their skills to the rising generation, thereby helping to maintain the fine tradition of British workmanship.

The sole ambition of many boys is to become a skilled craftsman, and for these young people the advantages of attendance at a secondary technical school speak for themselves. Occasionally, a boy will find that he has no aptitude for practical work. Even in such cases, the school has served a useful purpose in preventing the young person from entering a trade, in which he would have been a failure, and in directing him along an alternative path, which should lead to success and a full and happy life.

(ii) ADMISSION

The age of admission depends on local conditions, and at the present time there are three main variations:

(*a*) By competitive examination at the same time and frequently under the same conditions as for the grammar schools. Candidates who reach a sufficiently high standard may have an opportunity to choose between the two types of schools, when it should be remembered that the secondary technical school is designed for a specific purpose, namely, to train young people who wish to enter industry, particularly on the craft side. It is therefore wise, in certain circumstances, to choose the secondary technical school.

(*b*) By competitive examination for candidates between 12 and 13 years of age.

(*c*) By competitive examination for candidates between 13 and 14 years of age.

When the Education Act is fully implemented, it is anticipated that selection for admission to all types of secondary schools will be at 11 +, and (*b*) and (*c*) will be eliminated.

(iii) DURATION OF COURSE

A considerable proportion of secondary technical school students will desire to become indentured apprentices. Most of the national schemes involve an apprenticeship of five years to be completed at the age of 21 years. It is therefore usual for the majority of the students to leave at approximately 16 years of age. Delay may be dangerous, since some firms are reluctant to take apprentices who are over 16. It will be explained in a later section that some secondary technical schools provide an extended course for selected students, who wish to take the G.C.E. These students may continue their studies until they are 18 years of age, after which they will probably embark on a professional or technological career.

(iv) CURRICULUM

All types of secondary schools are under obligation to provide a sound balanced education, and in consequence the secondary technical school student occupies a considerable proportion of his time in the study of English, History, Geography, Current Affairs, etc., thereby preparing himself to live a full life as a member of a democratic society. Much more time, however, is spent on practical work than is the case in other types of secondary schools. Theoretical subjects closely allied to the crafts, particularly practical geometry and technical drawing, play an important part. Organization of courses varies considerably in different areas, and is influenced by local industries. Arrangements for a three-year course taking an annual entry of sixty boys at 12–13 years of age might be as follows:

Three classes are formed, and in the first year all follow the same syllabus. At the end of the first year, some sort of specialization begins, and three groups of twenty are formed with separate time-tables. Group A will take a general course, group B a building course, and group C an engineering course. The general course is designed for pupils who have shown in their first year considerable aptitude for more academic work (i.e. 'book work'). They are the sort of boys who wish to become architects, surveyors, designers, etc., or who may eventually take various competitive examinations for admission to certain sections of the Armed Forces. In some areas the syllabus is arranged to cover the requirements for the G.C.E. Accommodation difficulties sometimes preclude the possibility of running a General Course, and secondary schools catering only for craft training are found in some districts. The door is still open, however, when the student leaves school and enters Further Education Classes. Students in groups B and C will normally wish to become indentured apprentices or to enter one of the many training schemes sponsored by large industrial firms.

The successful craft teacher inspires his pupil to produce

only the best and to take pride in his work. In the initial stages the boy will work in as many types of material as circumstances permit, all the instruction being based on disciplinary exercises of a simple nature with emphasis on traditional methods. The varying materials used will give him that 'feel' of the medium so difficult to define but essential to true craftsmanship. Knowledge of all types of materials commonly used enables the specialist craftsman to understand and appreciate the work of others. After he has completed his introductory course, the boy will proceed to learn his chosen craft. If he intends to become an engineer he will receive instruction in bench work, turning, drilling, milling, and forging. The bricklayer will become reasonably proficient in the construction of walls, fireplaces, arches, etc., using the various types of brick. Plumbers will learn to do work in lead and copper sheet, 'wipe' joints and weld steel pipe. After instruction in the various types of joints, the carpenter will produce sections of doors, window frames, staircases, cupboards, etc.

Apart from the courses already described, in some areas where there is a high concentration of a staple industry, appropriate craft training is provided. For example, in Northamptonshire, secondary technical schools specializing in boot and shoe manufacture have been established for many years. Students receive practical instruction in workshops equipped with machines of the latest design and have excellent opportunities for advancement in local factories. In commercial schools, shorthand and typing may justifiably be called 'crafts'. The touch typist reaches a high state of proficiency by learning to type rhythmically with the aid of a series of gramophone records in graded speeds, and modern methods of shorthand teaching produce useful speeds in a short time.

Whatever may be the chosen career, the boy or girl will leave school with a clear knowledge of what is ahead and confidence in his or her ability to succeed.

(v) LEAVING SCHOOL

The boy of 15–16 years of age who enters a trade must be certain that the conditions of employment will lead him to become a qualified technician. If he enters the building trade, it is essential to find an employer who is giving full support to the training scheme of the Building Apprenticeship and Training Council, which culminates in a 'certificate of completion' at the end of the apprenticeship. Failure to do this may lead to recognition only as a labourer. Boys entering the motor vehicle repairing industry must likewise find an employer who insists on indenturing his young people under the scheme set out by the National Joint Industrial Council of the Motor Vehicle Retail and Repairing Trade. This will prevent the boy entering a dead-end job and will ensure that he has experience in all departments, instead of spending most of his time in unskilled work. Conditions in mechanical engineering vary according to the district, but a legal apprenticeship or well-defined training scheme should be insisted on. In all cases, the greatest possible use should be made of the Youth Employment Office, where appropriate literature and local information may be obtained.

It can be regarded as a general rule that every worthwhile apprenticeship or training scheme involves release by the employer for one day per week at the technical college at least up to the age of 18. The maximum benefit of a secondary technical school education can only be derived by an immediate transfer to Further Education

Classes. The principal or head of department of the college will advise on the most suitable course to be taken. In most cases the course will involve attendance for one day and two or more evenings per week and will lead up to an appropriate qualifying examination such as the National Certificate or Final Examinations of the City and Guilds of London Institute. Apprentices are normally deferred from military service for the full apprenticeship period.

Students from the first group of the secondary technical school (see p. 47) will probably aim for a career which does not ultimately involve work at the bench. They may find themselves in drawing offices, design or administrative work. Prospects are excellent for the boy with ambition. Higher National Certificates in Mechanical or Electrical Engineering lead under certain conditions to Associate Membership of the Institutions of Mechanical or Electrical Engineers respectively. A student possessing a National Certificate may also be eligible for a state scholarship, and, if he is suitable, proceed to a university. Students, who require the G.C.E. for the purpose of entering the professions, may usually take appropriate classes at the technical college.

One word of warning in regard to choice of course—as already indicated, aptitudes differ. One boy may be a genius on the bench and enjoy every minute when he is working with his tools. Another is happy only with a slide-rule, tee-square and drawing board, but is 'all thumbs' in the workshop. Students who are born craftsmen should attend a craft course and not eat out their hearts in attempting to pass National Certificates or similar examinations.

(vi) FUTURE DEVELOPMENT

At present the majority of technical schools follow the lines of the old junior technical school, and the information already given is therefore descriptive of them. Many local authorities have, however, already established the new type of secondary technical school envisaged by the Education Act, with a full five year course leading to the General Certificate of Education, and in some cases even a Sixth Form preparing pupils for the universities.

In these schools the information already provided remains true for some of the pupils. For many, however, the course resembles closely that of the grammar school. English Literature, Art, History, Geography, a Modern Language, Mathematics and the Sciences are taught (see Grammar School Curriculum, pp. 18–34). In addition the course provides such subjects as Engineering Drawing, Commerce, Workshop Practice, Metal and Wood Work, up to the General Certificate level. For those pupils whose career will not demand Matriculation the modern language will generally be omitted and the time spent on craft work.

In the Sixth Form emphasis is laid on Mathematics, Chemistry, Physics, Engineering and Commerce. Ultimately sufficient highly trained pupils should emerge to create a widespread tradition of Sixth Form work in the technical school.

CHAPTER 7

THE SECONDARY MODERN SCHOOL

(i) CURRICULUM

The modern school is responsible for the secondary education of the large majority of children and provides a general preparation for a wide field of employment in industry, commerce, agriculture, etc., whether skilled or unskilled. With this end in view, the essential requirement is a good standard of general education, the individual standard being determined by the individual potential of the pupil.

The provision of evening classes or part-time day release classes at the technical colleges presupposes a sound, basic education, from which the modern school pupil can proceed smoothly to further education. For this purpose a thorough grounding in English and Mathematics is particularly important. In more general terms the ability of the student to pursue effectively his ultimate career, to use profitably his leisure and to exercise wisely the privileges of citizenship is affected by his control of these subjects.

English and Mathematics are, therefore, of overriding importance in the curriculum of the modern school, and the methods of instruction are similar to those already outlined in the chapter on the grammar school.

Apart from these subjects, as the modern school is comparatively free from the demands of external examinations, it can select its curriculum from a very wide range of subjects, the following being most commonly studied.

English Subjects. History, Geography, Civics, Current Affairs, and Divinity.

Sciences. Elementary Physics, including Electricity, Magnetism, Light, Mechanics; Elementary Chemistry; and Elementary Biology comprising chiefly study of flora, fauna, the human body and its functions, hygiene.

Art and Craft. A wide range of media, e.g. line, colour, lino, design, drawing, bookbinding, needlework, lace, rug-making, puppetry, scenery, etc.

Woodwork. All types, including use of lathes, french polishing, etc.

Metalwork. Including light engineering, use of lathes, shapers, etc.

Technical Drawing. Including all forms of projection and the use of blue-prints.

Commercial Subjects. Commercial Arithmetic, Commercial English, Shorthand, Typing.

Music. Vocal and instrumental.

Domestic Science. Housecraft, Cookery, Hygiene, etc.

Gardening.

French. Usually restricted to selected pupils.

Physical Training and Games.

As the modern school necessarily includes in its intake a proportion of backward pupils, much of the work in English Subjects, Mathematics and the Sciences reinforces earlier instruction in reading, writing, comprehension and expression, thus performing a dual service.

For the better pupils, however, specialization is encouraged in the last year or so of the course, and, before leaving school, some pupils may have taken the elementary or intermediate examinations of the Royal Society for the Encouragement of Arts, Manufactures and Commerce, London (R.S.A.), or the Senior First Examination of the Educational Union (S.I.), or the G.C.E. (Ordinary Level). Where this involves remaining at school beyond the statutory leaving age maintenance allowances may be obtained in cases of hardship (see pp. 80–81).

These examinations lead directly by way of further education to the ultimate goal of the National and Higher National Certificates or the City and Guilds of London Institute Examinations.

There is thus a clearly defined educational path, embracing the modern school and the evening class or part-time day release scheme of the technical college, which can bring the student to a high level of attainment. This is equally true for both boys and girls, but for the latter the modern school also offers special courses such as the Pre-Nursing Course.

In some areas the policy is to create a bi-lateral form of secondary education, comprising modern and technical schools, with an easy flow of pupils from the one to the other. This greatly facilitates the prospect of specialized training for the suitable pupil.

Outside the normal curriculum the modern school is rapidly increasing the variety of its out-of-school activities, and the hobbies, clubs and cultural societies familiar to grammar school life are now undertaken by the modern schools.

(ii) EQUIPMENT

The eventual equipment of the modern schools will be closely allied to that of the grammar and technical schools. The science laboratories will be comprehensively equipped for the work which they undertake, and the domestic science rooms provided with modern gas and electric ovens, washing machines and domestic appliances. School buildings will include library, gymnasium and assembly hall with stage.

Considerable use is made of visual aids, the apparatus for which comprises sound film projectors, film-strip projectors, epidiascopes, microprojectors, daylight projection screens. Other equipment includes radiograms, wireless relay systems, and occasionally television.

(iii) TRAINING FOR CAREERS

Social training, discipline and behaviour are of especial importance in the modern schools, as this aspect of school life shapes ultimately the attitude of society itself. The passage of the pupil from school into the adult world may be smooth or difficult, and much experimental work has been and inevitably will be done on this subject.

It is clearly desirable that the transition should occur without either emotional disturbance to the pupil or irritation to others. To achieve this, the pupil must have acquired self-discipline, initiative and a healthy, constructive curiosity with respect to the world about him.

It has already been seen that the aim of the modern school is to ensure a reasonable standard of general education to which is added, by reason of the nature of the course studied, a fairly high level of manual dexterity.

In addition, therefore, to the advantage of specialized work, such as Metalwork, Woodwork, Technical Drawing, Commercial Studies, Pre-Nursing Training, etc., the pupil undergoes a general training freely adaptable to a wide field of employment.

Towards the end of the school career vocational guidance is provided by visits to local industry and by talks and interviews given by the Youth Employment Service. The pupil's school record features prominently in any consideration of the choice of employment.

During the pupil's last term at school prospective leavers are enabled to attend evening classes, and every encouragement is given to the pursuit of further education.

CHAPTER 8

THE SCHOOL HEALTH SERVICE

This service endeavours to cover the physical, mental and general well-being of the child throughout its school life.

Routine medical examinations of children are carried out during their school life at the following times:

First age group—as soon as possible after admission to school.

Second age group—at 10 years of age.

Third age group—during the last year at school.

In addition 13-year-old children at grammar and high schools are examined.

Special examinations. These are made at the same time as routine school inspection is being carried out, and they will frequently cater for children who at a previous examination were found to have some complaint and were marked down to be seen again at subsequent visits to the school. Also included are children whose parents request a special examination, or those referred by the head teacher or class teacher for some defect noted at school. All such examinations are confidential.

Routine examinations. The Medical Officer of Health is also usually the School Medical Officer. The work of school medical inspections is carried out by Assistant School Medical Officers assisted by Health Visitors.

When arrangements are made for the school medical inspection, parents are notified and requested to be present. They are also supplied with a form on which the previous medical history of the child is to be given. It is advisable that the parent should be present at such examinations. Thus the parent, the doctor and the health visitor, acting in conjunction, and having at their disposal the previous medical history, the home environment and the child's reaction to school life, are capable of acting in the best interests of that child.

The School Health Department arranges for the medical inspections at the different schools in the area, and each child has a medical card, Form 12 M, Ministry of Education. The results of all medical examinations are written on these forms, and a complete history of the child while at school is thus kept.

If a child leaves one school to attend a second, the school medical card is forwarded so that, when examined at this new school, the records of previous examinations are available for the School Medical Officer.

At the medical examination any complaint discovered is noted down, and, depending on what this complaint may be, one of the following requests may be made:

(i) Cases may be referred to the family doctor for further investigation or treatment.

(ii) Request may be made for the child to be seen by a specialist. If this is done the family doctor must be informed and his consent obtained first. Reports by specialists are sent to the family doctor with a copy for the School Health Department to be attached to the child's record card. This means that at subsequent examinations the School Medical Officer will have available the report from the specialist.

The procedure adopted with regard to the above is as follows. The request is made on the school medical card which is returned to the School Health Department. The School Medical Officer arranges the appointments, and parents are notified as to the date and place where the child is to be examined.

The following services are available for the school child, if some defect is discovered at the medical inspection:

(*a*) *Minor ailment clinics*. These clinics deal with minor abrasions, re-dressing of wounds, minor skin complaints, etc. At such clinics a health visitor is in attendance.

(*b*) *Dental clinic*. Cases referred to this clinic are seen by the school dentist and his staff, who may provide the following treatment: extractions, fillings, scalings, ortho-dontia. At such a centre, also, education in dental hygiene may be provided.

(*c*) *Ophthalmic services*. Children with defective vision, squint, etc., are referred to the ophthalmic surgeon. At such clinics, refractions, treatment of squint, etc., are carried out.

(*d*) *Ear, nose and throat clinic*. Children found to have some defect of hearing, enlarged tonsils and adenoids, nasal obstruction, or any defect that falls under this heading, are referred to this clinic, where they are examined by the E.N.T. specialist.

(*e*) *Consultant services*. Special defects found at medical examinations may require further investigation and the opinion of a specialist in that particular branch of medicine, e.g. a child found to have a congenital heart murmur requiring further investigation may be referred to a cardiac specialist, while a second child with a respiratory disease would be referred to a chest physician.

(*f*) *Speech therapy*. Children found at school medical examinations to have speech defects, stammers, stutters, can be referred for special treatment. These clinics are set up by the school health department at convenient centres and deal with the children in any one area.

(g) *Orthopaedic clinic.* Any child discovered to have any deformity of the spine, thorax, or limbs, is referred to this clinic for the opinion of the orthopaedic surgeon and treatment.

(h) *Mental health.* This department is concerned with the ascertainment of mental defects and deals with intelligence testing and the attendance of children at child guidance clinics. The department in recent years has shown a very great increase in its activities and field covered. The school health services employ an educational psychologist and usually have the services of a psychiatrist. Intelligence testing is carried out by either the educational psychologist or the assistant school medical officer, who have been trained in this particular type of work and approved by the Ministry.

In the examination of the school child great importance must be paid to any defect of vision or hearing. Often it is found that, prior to the discovery of such defects, the child has never mentioned these, and even at times would appear to be unconscious of them. Such defects may be the cause of backwardness at school, owing to the fact that the child is unable to see the blackboard or hear the teacher. An important part of all school medical examinations is the testing of vision and of hearing.

One cannot over-emphasize the value of the School Medical Services. Often when examining entrants the doctor is giving a child its first complete medical examination. Parents may have thought previously that there was no reason to have the child examined by their own family doctor, and yet at such examinations, time and time again, some defect will be found that previously had not been noticed by the parents. Early diagnosis and treatment may mean that the child will be able to carry out the full activities that go with a normal school life. On the other hand if some heart complaint is discovered, or something else of a serious nature, the activities of the child may have to be curtailed.

The main functions of the School Health Services are to safeguard the child during this period of its life, and to see that the child is maintained in a healthy physical and mental condition during its school life, and is thus able to obtain full benefit from it.

School meals. Since the introduction of this service a great advance has been noted in the nutrition of schoolchildren. It helps to safeguard their diet, and it has often been found that difficult feeders improve when they eat in the company of their school friends. This service is also of considerable assistance to the mothers of large families. In the past it has been found, owing to wrong feeding or to underfeeding at home, that some children have not developed physically as well as their schoolmates. With school meals such children are given the same opportunity for physical development. School meals also present an opportunity of improving the child's standards of hygiene with regard to the taking of a meal. The importance of personal cleanliness and the proper use of cutlery can be taught.

Physical education. The importance of this side of school life has come very much to the fore in recent years. A healthy body helps the child in his school life, and so this should not be neglected. Postural defects, flat feet, etc. can conveniently be treated by the Physical Training Instructor at school, and so there should be liaison between this teacher and the school doctor. Notification of pupils who should not be allowed to do strenuous exercises is passed to the head teacher. Frequently, however, such cases can take physical exercises in moderation, and this must be stressed. To prevent children completely from taking part in such activities is not in their best interests. If they can do certain things in moderation, they should be allowed to do so. Team games help in the formation of character, and a physically fit pupil with a team spirit will make a good citizen when school days are finished.

Special schools for handicapped and delicate children

The education authority in co-operation with the school health service is responsible for vacancies for children in the following types of school:

(1) Open-air schools for delicate children.

(2) Special schools for educationally sub-normal children. At such schools specially trained teachers are employed and individual attention can be given.

(3) Schools for physically handicapped children. At such schools a child, who is so physically handicapped as to be unable to take part in normal school life, is specially catered for.

CHAPTER 9

CAREERS

This section indicates briefly the educational standard required for entry to various careers and the addresses from which further information may be obtained. Where the G.C.E. is required the following symbols are used:

E = English.	Sc = A science.
H = History.	Ch = Chemistry.
G = Geography.	Ph = Physics.
M = Mathematics.	F = A foreign language.
GSc = General Science.	

Unless the word 'advanced' is used, it may be assumed that the Ordinary Level is required. +1, +2, etc. = additional passes required in unspecified subjects.

The Youth Employment Service, working in close connexion with the schools, provides ample information about careers, not only locally but throughout the country. For school-leavers of ability, who accept posts away from home and have to pay for their lodging, the Ministry of Labour can make a 'Special Aptitude Grant' to supplement salary. Application should be made to the local Youth Employment Officer.

BOYS

ACCOUNTANCY. E, M, +3 *or* E, M (one at advanced) +2.

(*a*) Institute of Chartered Accountants in England and Wales, Moorgate Place, E.C.2.

(*b*) Society of Incorporated Accountants and Auditors, Victoria Embankment, W.C.2.

ACTUARIAL WORK. E, M+3.
Institute of Actuaries, Staple Inn Buildings, W.C. 1.

ADVERTISING. E+3.
(a) Advertising Association, Ludgate House, 110–111 Fleet Street, E.C. 4.
(b) Institute of Incorporated Practitioners in Advertising, 48 Russell Square, W.C. 1.

AGRICULTURE, HORTICULTURE AND DAIRYING. Sound general education plus practical experience for admission to Farm Institutes or Institutes of Agriculture. University degree required for teaching or research work.
(a) National Agricultural Examination Board, 16 Bedford Square, W.C. 1.
(b) National Dairy Examination Board, 16 Bedford Square, W.C. 1.
(c) National Poultry Diploma Examination Board, The Bungalow, Chilworth, Surrey.
(d) Royal Horticultural Society, Vincent Square, S.W. 1.
(e) Agricultural Research Council, Cunard Buildings, 15 Regent Street, W. 1.

ARCHITECTURE. E, M+3 or E, M+2 (if one is advanced).
Royal Institute of British Architects, 66 Portland Place, W. 1.

ART AND DESIGN. Sound general education + specialized training, aptitude and artistic ability.
The Society of Industrial Artists, 7 Woburn Square, W.C. 1.
The Council of Industrial Design, Tilbury House, Petty France, S.W. 1.

AUCTIONEERING AND ESTATE AGENCY. E, M+2.
The Incorporated Society of Auctioneers and Landed Property Agents, 34 Queen's Gate, S.W. 7.

BAKING AND FLOUR CONFECTIONERY. No standard educational qualifications. Apprenticeship scheme. Full-time course of training available.

The National Joint Apprenticeship Council for the Baking Industry, 1 Buckingham Palace Gardens, Buckingham Palace Road, Westminster, S.W.1.

The National Board for Bakery Education. Address as above.

BANKING. G.C.E. preferably with E, M+2.

Institute of Bankers, 11 Birchin Lane, E.C.3.

BLACKSMITHING AND FARRIERY. No standard educational qualifications. Apprenticeship scheme. Full-time training course available at College of Rural Crafts.

BREWING. E, M, Sc+2 or Technical or other training.

Institute of Brewing, Goring Hotel, Grosvenor Gardens, S.W.1.

BUILDING:

(a) *Craftsmen* (carpenters, bricklayers, plumbers, painters and decorators, etc.). No standard educational qualifications. Apprenticeship scheme.

(b) *Managerial, executive and technical posts.* Entry possible from all types of education+technical and professional training.

The Institute of Builders, 48 Bedford Square, W.C.1.

The Institute of Clerks of Works of Great Britain Inc. General Secretary W. J. Gibbins, 5 Broughton Road, Thornton Heath, Surrey.

The Institution of Municipal and County Engineers, 84 Eccleston Square, S.W.1.

CATERING MANAGEMENT. Good general education, to G.C.E. standard+apprenticeship *or* full-time training at technical college or hotel school.

The Hotel and Catering Institute, 24 Portman Square, W.1.

CHEMISTRY (Industrial, Analytical *or* Research). E, M, Sc. The Institute of Chemistry, 30 Russell Square, W.C.1.

CHIROPODY. Good general education + special training. The Society of Chiropodists, 21 Cavendish Square, W.1.

CHURCH WORK (clerical and lay workers). Necessary educational qualifications and training vary considerably between the various denominations. A strong sense of vocation is essential.

CIVIL SERVICE:
(*a*) Four general classes recruited by open competition (home and foreign service).
(*b*) Specialist classes, e.g. lawyers, scientists—recruitment usually by competitive interview.
  The Civil Service Commission, Burlington Gardens, W.1.
  The Civil Service Commission, Scientific Branch, 7th Floor, Trinidad House, Old Burlington Street, W.1.

COAL MINING. No standard educational qualifications; special training scheme at National Coal Board Training Centre and part-time attendance at Technical College.

COLLIERY MANAGEMENT:
Entry (*a*) University degree or diploma course in mining.
Or (*b*) Sound general education followed by part-time study at a mining school and technical college while working underground.

DANCING. Good general education + specialized training. The Royal Academy of Dancing, 154 Holland Park Avenue, W.11.

DENTISTRY. E, M *or* Sc, F + 2 + full-time training course at dental school, equivalent to university degree. The British Dental Association, 13 Hill Street, Berkeley Square, W.1.

DISPENSING. E, M + 3.

The Pharmaceutical Society of Great Britain, 17 Blooms-bury Square, W.C. 1.

DRAMATIC ART. Good general education + specialized training. Academic qualifications necessary for teaching.

The Royal Academy of Dramatic Art, 62 Gower Street, W.C. 1.

The Central School of Speech Training and Dramatic Art, Royal Albert Hall, Kensington, S.W. 7.

The Guildhall School of Music and Drama, John Carpenter Street, Victoria Embankment, E.C. 4.

The Old Vic Theatre School, Waterloo Road, S.E. 1.

The British Drama League, 9 Fitzroy Square, W. 1.

DRAUGHTSMANSHIP:

(a) Engineering. Good English and Maths. Workshop training essential.

(b) Building, *see* Architecture and Building.

(c) Cartography, *see* Civil Service and Surveying.

ECONOMICS. Honours degree course.

ELECTRICIAN (maintenance work, wireman, etc.). No standard educational qualifications. Apprenticeship scheme.

ENGINEERING (aeronautical, automobile, electrical, marine, mechanical, etc.). Broadly there are three methods of entry:

(a) Craft apprenticeship. No standard educational qualifications required.

(b) Engineering apprenticeship. G.C.E. standard, M and E necessary.

(c) Student apprenticeship. Full-time training at university or technical college in preparation for a degree, with sandwich courses.

The Institution of Mechanical Engineers, Storey's Gate, St James's Park, S.W. 1.

The Royal Aeronautical Society, 4 Hamilton Place, W. 1.

The Institution of Heating and Ventilating Engineers, 72–74 Victoria Street, S.W. 1.

The Institution of Locomotive Engineers, 28 Victoria Street, S.W. 1.

The Institute of Marine Engineers, 85 Minories, E.C. 3.

The Institution of Production Engineers, 36 Portman Square, W. 1.

FORESTRY. *Foresters.* Practical experience + training in forestry school at the age of 19. Competitive examination and selection board. *Forest Officers.* University degree or diploma in forestry.

The Forestry Commission, 25 Savile Row, W. 1.

GEOLOGY. First or good second class honours degree.

HAIRDRESSING. No standard educational qualifications. Five years apprenticeship *or* full-time training courses available.

Incorporated Guild of Hairdressers, Wigmakers and Perfumiers, 33 Great Queen Street, W.C. 2.

H.M. FORCES. Competitive examinations at various educational levels for entry to Navy, Army and Air Force.

The Admiralty, London, S.W. 1.

The War Office, London, S.W. 1.

The Royal Air Force, Victory House, Kingsway, W.C. 2.

The Civil Service Commission (for Naval cadetships—special entry, entry to Sandhurst and to Cranwell College).

HORSE-RIDING (jockeys, stable-boys, etc.). No standard educational qualifications. Apprenticeship scheme for jockeys.

HOSPITAL ADMINISTRATION. E, M.

Institute of Hospital Administrators, Tavistock Square, W.C. 1.

HOTEL WORK. *See* Catering.

HOUSING MANAGEMENT:
  (a) G.C.E. + part-time study. (b) University degree.
  The Society of Housing Managers (Incorporated), 13 Suffolk Street, Pall Mall, S.W. 1.
  The Institute of Housing (Incorporated), 359 Strand, W.C. 2.

INSURANCE. E, M + 2.
  The Chartered Insurance Institute, 20 Aldermanbury, E.C. 2.
  The Corporation of Insurance Brokers, 3 St Helen's Place, E.C. 3.

INTERIOR DECORATING. Good general education + specialized full-time training.
  The Incorporated Institute of British Decorators, Drayton House, Gordon Street, W.C. 1.

IRON AND STEEL. No standard educational qualifications. Apprenticeship schemes with part-time technical college training.
  Training Department, British Iron and Steel Federation, 46 Victoria Street, S.W. 1.

JOURNALISM. E, shorthand and typing necessary. No recognized professional examinations.
  The Institute of Journalists, 2 and 4 Tudor Street, E.C. 4.
  The National Union of Journalists, 7 John Street, W.C. 1.

LAND AGENCY. E, M + 2.
  The Land Agents' Society, 329 High Holborn, W.C. 1.

LAUNDRY MANAGEMENT. Ch, Ph. One year's practical experience, then 2-year full-time training course or employment with part-time study.
  The Institute of British Launderers Ltd., 16–17 Lancaster Gate, W. 2.

LAW. *Solicitors:* E, H, Latin + 2.

The Law Society, Chancery Lane, W.C. 2.

The Law Society of Scotland, Law Society's Hall, Bank Street, Edinburgh.

Barristers: G.C.E. at university entrance level, including Advanced English and Advanced Latin.

The Council of Legal Education, 7 Stone Buildings, W.C. 2.

LIBRARIANSHIP. E + 4 *or* E + 2 + an advanced subject. F is desirable.

The Library Association, Chaucer House, Malet Place, W.C. 1.

LOCAL GOVERNMENT SERVICE. General Entry—E, M + 2. Professional and Technical Departments (e.g. Surveyor's), specialized training.

Local Government Examinations Board, 37 Upper Grosvenor Street, W. 1.

MEDICAL LABORATORY TECHNOLOGY. E, Ch *or* GSc, M + 1.

Institute of Medical Laboratory Technology, 9 Harley Street, W. 1.

MEDICINE AND SURGERY. University or School of Medicine degree course.

The British Medical Association, B.M.A. House, Tavistock Square, W.C. 1.

MERCHANT NAVY. Necessary educational qualifications and training varies according to branch of service or occupation, e.g. engineers, radio officers, deck ratings, stewards, etc.

Shipping Federation Ltd., 52 Leadenhall Street, E.C. 3.

Ministry of Transport, Berkeley Square House, W. 1.

METALLURGY. Ch, Ph, M + 3.

The Institution of Metallurgists, 4 Grosvenor Gardens, S.W. 1.

The Institution of Mining and Metallurgy, Salisbury House, Finsbury Circus, E.C. 2.

METEOROLOGY. M, Ph.

Meteorological Department, Air Ministry, Kingsway, W.C. 2.

MOTOR MECHANIC, VEHICLE REPAIRER, ETC. No standard educational qualifications. Apprenticeship scheme.

MUSIC. Good general education + specialized training. G.C.E. standard required for teacher training and certain qualifications, e.g. Senior Diploma of the Royal College of Music.

NURSING. Good general education. Training commences at $17\frac{1}{2}$–18 years of age.

Nursing Appointments Office, Ministry of Labour and National Service, 23 Portland Square, W. 1.

OCCUPATIONAL THERAPY. E, Sc + 3.

The Association of Occupational Therapy, 251 Brompton Road, S.W. 3.

OPTICS. E, M, Sc.

The British Optical Association, 65 Brook Street, W. 1.

The National Association of Opticians, 130 Princes Road, Liverpool 8.

The Scottish Association of Opticians, 121 Bath Street, Glasgow, C. 2.

The Worshipful Company of Spectacle Makers, Apothecaries' Hall, Blackfriars Lane, E.C. 4.

The Association of Dispensing Opticians, 36 Cavendish Square, W. 1.

ORTHOPTICS. E and 3 selected Science subjects.

The Orthoptic Board, Midgarth, Oxshott, Surrey.

PATENT AGENCY. University degree in Science or Engineering desirable.

Chartered Institute of Patent Agents, Staple Inn Buildings, W.C. 1.

PERSONNEL MANAGEMENT. Good general standard of education. No one recognized method of training. Possibilities include degree course + Social Science training *or* Social Science diploma.

The Institute of Labour Management, Aldwych House, W.C. 2.

PHARMACY. E, M, F + 2.

The Pharmaceutical Society of Great Britain, 17 Bloomsbury Square, W.C. 1.

PHOTOGRAPHY. Good general standard of education + training in a school of photography.

The Royal Photographic Society, 16 Princes Gate, S.W. 7.

PHYSICS. University degree course.

PHYSIOTHERAPY. Ch, Ph + 2.

The Chartered Society of Physiotherapy, Tavistock House (South), Tavistock Square, W.C. 1.

PLASTICS. M, Sc.

The Plastics Institute, Adelphi Buildings, Adam Street, W.C. 2.

POLICE. Good general standard of education. Minimum age of entry 22 years.

Police Recruiting Department, Home Office, Whitehall, S.W. 1.

Police Recruiting Department, Scottish Home Department, St Andrew's House, Edinburgh.

PRINTING AND BOOKBINDING. No standard educational qualifications. Apprenticeship scheme.

The Joint Industrial Council of the Printing and Allied Trades of Great Britain and Ireland, 11 Bedford Row, W.C. 1.

PRISON SERVICE. G.C.E. or entrance examination.

The Establishment Officer, Prison Commission, Horseferry House, Dean Ryle Street, Westminster, S.W. 1.

The Director of Prison and Borstal Services, Scottish Home Department, 29 St Andrew Square, Edinburgh 2.

PSYCHOLOGY. University degree course.

PUBLISHING:

Entry (*a*) As junior clerical assistant, apprentice, etc. (*see* Printing and Bookbinding). No standard educational qualifications.

(*b*) For higher posts. University degree, particularly in English Literature *or* Classics.

RAILWAY (clerical and technical posts). G.C.E. entrance exam. Other Departments (e.g. Workshops, Permanent Way, Signal and Telegraph). No standard educational qualification. Apprenticeship scheme.

RETAIL DISTRIBUTION. Grocery and Provisions, Outfitting, Stationery, etc. No standard educational qualifications.

RURAL CRAFTS (e.g. Wheelwrighting, Agricultural Engineering, Property Maintenance. No standard educational qualifications. Full-time training courses available.

SALES MANAGEMENT AND SALESMANSHIP. No standard educational qualifications. Training with firm + part-time study at technical college, etc.

Incorporated Sales Managers Association, 23 Bedford Square, S.W. 1.

SECRETARIAL WORK. Sound general education—E and M important + commercial training and specialized study.

The Corporation of Certified Secretaries, Secretaries Hall, 28 Fitzroy Square, W. 1.

The Chartered Institute of Secretaries, 16 George Street, Mansion House, E.C. 4.

SHIPBROKING. No standard educational qualifications. Training within the firm. G.C.E. (4 subjects) required for admission to Intermediate Examination of Institute of Chartered Shipbrokers.

SOCIAL WORK. Approved Schools, Mental Health Work, Probation Officer, etc. G.C.E. (4 subjects) + specialized training.

SPEECH THERAPY. G.C.E. (4 subjects) + specialized training.

SURVEYING. E, M, H *or* G, + 2.
   The Royal Institution of Chartered Surveyors, 12 Great George Street, Westminster, S.W. 1.

TEACHING. G.C.E. (5 subjects). Course at teacher's training college or university.

TOWN AND COUNTRY PLANNING. E, M, F + 2, or previous qualification in another subject, e.g. Surveying or Geography.
   The Town Planning Institute, 18 Ashley Place, Victoria, S.W. 1.

TRAVEL AGENCY. No standard educational qualifications or methods of training. Languages and commercial training useful.

TRICHOLOGY. Good general standard of education + specialized training. Experience in a hairdressing establishment is useful.
   The Institute of Trichologists, 53 South Molton Street, W. 1.

VETERINARY SCIENCE. Full-time training at veterinary school. Entrance qualification equivalent to university entrance.
   The Royal College of Veterinary Surgeons, 9–10 Red Lion Square, W.C. 1.

WHOLESALE TEXTILE TRADE. Clerks, stock-keepers, salesmen, travellers, buyers, etc. No standard educational qualifications.

Wholesale Textile Association, 75 Cannon Street, E.C.4.

YOUTH LEADERSHIP. Social Science or Teacher training or special university course.

GIRLS

ACCOUNTANCY. *See* Boys List.

ADVERTISING. *See* Boys List.

AIR HOSTESS. Good general standard of education + nursing training.

B.O.A.C., Airways House, Great West Road, Brentford, Middlesex.

B.E.A.C., Keyline House, Ruislip, Middlesex.

ALMONER. Science subject, E + 3. Social Science training + specialized training.

The Institute of Almoners, Tavistock House (North), Tavistock Square, W.C.1.

ARCHITECTURE. *See* Boys List.

ART AND DESIGN. *See* Boys List.

BANKING. *See* Boys List. Educational qualifications can be lower for shorthand-typist and machine-operator posts.

BOOK-KEEPING. No standard educational qualifications. Commercial training necessary.

CATERING MANAGEMENT. *See* Boys List.

CHILD WELFARE. *See* Social Work.

CHIROPODY. *See* Boys List.

CHURCH WORK. *See* Boys List.

CIVIL SERVICE. *See* Boys List.

CORSETRY. No standard educational qualifications; full-time training courses available.

DAIRYING. *See* Agriculture, etc. (Boys List).

DANCING. *See* Boys List.

DENTISTRY. *See* Boys List.

DIETETICS. Degree course, Teacher training or S.R.N. + specialized training.
   The British Dietetic Association, 251 Brompton Road, S.W. 3.

DISPENSING. *See* Boys List.

DOMESTIC SCIENCE:
   (*a*) Teaching: degree course or training college course.
   (*b*) Large-scale catering: domestic science college or technical training college course.
   (*c*) Demonstrating: domestic science training college course + specialized training.

DOMESTIC WORK. No standard educational qualifications. Full-time training course available.
   National Institute of Houseworkers, 53 Mount Street, London, W. 1.

DRAMATIC ART. *See* Boys List.

DRESSMAKING AND MILLINERY. No standard educational qualifications. Apprenticeship schemes. Full-time training courses available.

EMBROIDERY. No standard educational qualifications. Full-time training courses.
   Royal School of Needlework, Exhibition Road, South Kensington, S.W. 7.

FAMILY CASEWORK. *See* Social Work (Boys List).

75

FLORAL ART. No standard educational qualifications. Apprenticeship scheme. Full-time training course available.

HAIRDRESSING AND BEAUTY CULTURE. No standard educational qualifications. Training given by apprenticeship or by a full-time course at a school of hairdressing and beauty culture.

H.M. FORCES. No standard educational qualifications. Volunteers accepted from the age of 17½ years.

HORTICULTURE. G.C.E. + practical experience for entry to farm institute or diploma course. Degree usually required for teaching posts.

HOSPITAL ADMINISTRATION. *See* Boys List.

HOTEL WORK. *See* Catering.

HOUSING MANAGEMENT. *See* Boys List.

INSURANCE. *See* Boys List.

JOURNALISM. *See* Boys List.

KENNEL WORK. No standard educational qualifications, or method of entry. Love of animals and of an open-air life essential.

LAUNDRY HANDS. No standard educational qualifications. Training within the firm as ironers, calender hands, sorters, etc.

LAUNDRY MANAGEMENT. *See* Boys List.

LAW. *See* Boys List.

LIBRARIANSHIP. *See* Boys List.

LOCAL GOVERNMENT SERVICE. General entry—usually E, M + 2.

MEDICAL LABORATORY TECHNOLOGY. *See* Boys List.

MEDICINE AND SURGERY. *See* Boys List.

MORAL WELFARE WORK. *See* Social Work (Boys List).

MUSIC. *See* Boys List.

N.A.A.F.I. No standard educational qualifications. Volunteers accepted from the age of 18 years.

NEIGHBOURHOOD WORK. *See* Social Work (Boys List).

NURSERY, NURSING. Good secondary educational standard. Training commences from 16 years. Full-time training courses at nursery, nurse training schools available.

NURSING AND MIDWIFERY. Good general education. Training usually commences at 17½–18 years. Some cadet schemes commence at 16 years.

Nursing Appointments Office, Ministry of Labour and National Service, 23 Portland Square, W. 1.

The Royal College of Midwives, 57 Lower Belgrave Street, S.W. 1.

The Central Midwives' Board, 73 Great Peter Street, S.W. 1.

OCCUPATIONAL THERAPY. *See* Boys List.

OPTICS. *See* Boys List.

ORTHOPTICS. *See* Boys List.

PERSONNEL MANAGEMENT. *See* Boys List.

PHARMACY. *See* Boys List.

PHYSIOTHERAPY. *See* Boys List.

POLICE. Good standard of general education. Minimum age of entry 22 years.

Police Recruiting Department, Home Office, Whitehall, S.W. 1.

Police Recruiting Department, Scottish Home Department, St Andrew's House, Edinburgh.

POULTRY REARING. Good general standard of education + practical experience for admission to Farm Institutes.

PRINTING AND BOOKBINDING. No standard educational qualifications. Learnership scheme.

PSYCHOLOGY. *See* Boys List.

PUBLISHING. *See* Boys List.

RADIOGRAPHY. Sc + M *or* S.R.N. *or* Diploma of the Chartered Society of Physiotherapy or Membership of the Pharmaceutical Society + specialized training.

RETAIL DISTRIBUTION. *See* Boys List.

SECRETARIAL WORK. *See* Boys List.

SHORTHAND TYPIST. No standard educational qualifications. Commercial training. Languages useful.

SOCIAL WORK. *See* Boys List.

SPEECH THERAPY. *See* Boys List.

TAILORING. No standard educational qualifications. Apprenticeship scheme. Full-time training courses available.

TEACHING. *See* Boys List.

TRAVEL AGENCY. *See* Boys List.

VETERINARY SCIENCE. *See* Boys List.

WAITRESS. No standard educational qualifications.

WHOLESALE TEXTILE TRADE. *See* Boys List.

WINDOW DRESSING. No standard educational qualifications. Full-time training course available.

YOUTH LEADERSHIP. *See* Boys List.

Other types of employment can be found in a variety of industries. Often these are somewhat localized, e.g. boot and shoe manufacture, leather dressing, pottery making, textiles, hosiery manufacture, carpet making, glove making, etc. The majority of these industries have good learnership or apprenticeship schemes.

Information regarding any type of employment can be obtained from the Youth Employment Officer.

The Youth Employment Service is available to all types of school leavers and has facilities for assisting older pupils with specialized qualifications.

CHAPTER 10

MISCELLANEOUS PROBLEMS

(i) PARENTS' EXPENSES

The chief outlay when a boy or girl enters the secondary school is on uniform and games kit. Local authorities are empowered by the Ministry of Education to make a grant covering the cost of the above, where parents' circumstances warrant it. In order to obtain this, parents should write to the Education Officer of their local committee for a form of application, on which they will be required to make a confidential statement of income.

In similar circumstances, school meals can be obtained without charge.

Except for minor incidentals, all other expenses are met by the local authority. Free transport, for example, is provided for pupils living three miles or more from the school.

The incidentals which parents have to pay may include a proportion of the travel expenses when a pupil is a member of a school team, a small annual subscription for school magazines and fixture cards, and the cost of school expeditions. Here again, there is usually a school fund for the assistance of needy pupils, and the headmaster or headmistress should be approached in cases of hardship.

Most schools have Parents' Associations which control their own funds and are always willing to give assistance.

Many schools also have second-hand clothing shops which are non-profit-making, and which considerably reduce the cost of equipping growing children.

When a pupil reaches the age of 15, application may be

made in cases of hardship for a maintenance allowance. The maximum annual allowance at age 15 is generally £15 or more, and at age 16 +, £25–£50.

Unfortunately, this is partly offset by the fact that the National Insurance Family Allowance is discontinued after the sixteenth birthday. The usual Income Tax Children's Allowance does, however, continue during the period of full-time education, including the university.

When within one year of the maximum compulsory school age, a pupil can with the school's agreement obtain permission from the Education Committee to take a part-time job. The number of hours worked and the conditions of employment are governed by local statute, so that a reasonable amount of leisure is guaranteed. A typical example: The maximum working time on school days is two hours, falling between 7–8 a.m. and 5–7 p.m. On school holidays the maximum is five hours between 7 a.m. and 7 p.m., and there must be a continuous recreation period of five hours.

(ii) THE PARENT-TEACHER ASSOCIATION

Many schools of all types have today Parent-Teacher Associations which form an admirable link between school and home, and from which both sides gain considerable benefit.

The parents gain by a closer acquaintance with educational problems and with the demands made on their children by the curriculum. They acquire a wider knowledge of the range of careers open to their children and of the qualifications required. They have easier access to individual members of the staff in an informal social atmosphere.

The teachers on the other hand derive by personal

contact with the parents a new understanding of their pupils and frequently gain an invaluable fund of local knowledge and conditions, which may otherwise be denied them.

Many practical aspects of school life demand the whole-hearted co-operation of the parents, and joint discussion frequently avoids misunderstandings over such thorny problems as school meals, transport, uniform, discipline, homework, etc. Moreover, a school can have no more ardent ally than its parents when it is anxious to raise funds for some amenity which might otherwise be beyond its reach.

It is sometimes forgotten that the boys' school with its masters naturally has a purely masculine outlook and, although functioning admirably in its own estimation, may fall sadly short in domestic matters of the standards which mothers approve. Similarly in the case of the girls' schools, the opinions of the fathers, however hesitant, may occasionally contain the seed of wisdom.

These associations are now so firmly established in the field of education that it is not unusual for the Parents' Association to have its own representative on the governing body of the school. A further development in some areas is the federation of local associations, thus creating a most powerful means of expression for parental opinion, which can make itself felt beyond the limits of purely local affairs.

(iii) SCHOOL UNIFORM

This is sometimes resented, more particularly by girls. Assuming that the uniform is reasonably attractive and not more expensive than other clothing of similar durability, the main argument advanced is that it stifles individuality and personal taste. There are, of course, many other ways in school life of expressing one's individuality, but apart from that there are sound reasons for the insistence on uniform.

(1) It reinforces the corporate spirit of the school.

(2) It is invaluable for recognition purposes during school expeditions, team travel, etc.

(3) It imposes on the pupil when in public a higher standard of responsibility and conduct than he might otherwise have, if only because, if he misbehaves, his school is readily identified and the school will probably be informed.

(4) It avoids in a school drawn from different social levels a class distinction made visible by clothing.

(5) Where the school has a second-hand clothing shop, the wearing of uniform can actually be cheaper than that of ordinary clothing.

(iv) HOMEWORK

Although there are no regulations governing homework, the average amount required of pupils in the grammar schools is usually:

Years 1–3. Maximum of 1 hour for 5 nights per week.

Years 4–5. Maximum of 1½ hours for 5 nights per week.

In the Sixth Form work is naturally heavier and depends on the programme of the individual student.

It is suggested from time to time that homework serves no useful purpose. Few schools would agree with this, although schoolmasters themselves do not regard the marking of homework as an outstanding attraction of the profession.

Homework is valuable because it gives the pupil the opportunity of (a) confronting problems on his own, (b) reading more widely about a subject. These could be done at school, but only at the expense of time more usefully allotted to instruction.

The chief enemies of homework are radio and television. Both are valuable, provided that it is remembered that activity is a vital part of true education. A pupil is better employed solving difficulties himself than watching others do so.

(v) HOBBIES AND SOCIETIES

Out-of-school activities are a vital part of school life, and the pupil who never arrives home late because of them is missing a great deal of value.

Typical activities for boys are combined cadet force, scouts, railway club, stamp club, aero-modelling club, debating society, photographic club, school orchestra and choir, dramatic society, scientific society, nature study club, puppetry, chess club.

And for girls, many of the above, and also guides, rangers, play-reading, etc.

All of these activities and many others foster the pupil's creative ability and self-confidence with consequent benefit to normal school work.

(vi) FOREIGN VISITS, EXCHANGES AND CORRESPONDENCE

Most schools organize parties to visit foreign countries. These serve to broaden the pupil's experience and outlook and are much cheaper than normal travel for the individual.

Group travel is unlikely, however, to improve greatly a student's knowledge of a foreign language. For this the best method is to arrange an exchange with a foreign student. This can be done through the school. The exchange can be simultaneous or consecutive, and the two students need not be of the same sex, if an alternative arrangement is better suited to the accommodation available. The cost is, of course, merely that of travel and passport.

A useful preliminary to an exchange is correspondence with a foreign student, which can also be arranged by the school.

(vii) PREMATURE LEAVING

When parents enter their child for the annual entrance examination they are sometimes required by the local education authority to sign a guarantee that, if a place at the grammar school is offered and accepted, they will keep the child at school until the end of the school year when he or she becomes 16.

That contract is occasionally broken, sometimes for unavoidable economic reasons, but sometimes merely because the pupil, seeing leavers from other types of school in full employment at the age of 15, is impatient to do likewise.

In the latter case parents should take a firm line in the pupil's own interest. It should be remembered that employers are well aware of the functions of grammar schools and of the General Certificate of Education. If a pupil has left school without completing the course, the natural conclusion is that the underlying reason was lack of ability to see that course to a successful finish.

Even when the premature leaver has employment awaiting him, it does not follow that he will always wish to remain in that particular employment.

The G.C.E. is positive evidence of training and ability and as such is a passport to a worthwhile career and remains a standby long after the pupil has left school.

Printed in the United States
By Bookmasters